About the Author

Toddy Hoare trained as a sculptor and was freelance for three years, until recession in the mid-1970s made such a living impossible. So he joined the 15/19th King's Royal Hussars to pay his debts, serving in Northern Ireland. Ordination followed via The Missions to Seamen in Holland and Wycliffe Hall, Oxford. After a curacy in Guisborough, he was the curate-in-charge of the Hillside Parishes in North Yorkshire on the Moors near Thirsk for twenty-five years. All those miscellaneous experiences proved useful during that quarter century amongst twelve villages with eight churches, with sculpture playing a prominent role, illustrating scripture or as sermons in bronze. When his wife, Liz, got a post she could not refuse teaching spiritual formation at Wycliffe Hall Theological College he retired to concentrate on sculpture once more and exhibit in London. He took up the pen to write poetry whose muse had been largely dormant since art school. He has four children, eight grandchildren, a Labrador, and as much enjoyment of Oxford as there had been of Yorkshire.

Sonnetry

Toddy Hoare

Sonnetry

Olympia Publishers
London

www.olympiapublishers.com
OLYMPIA PAPERBACK EDITION

ISBN: 978-1-78830-009-4

First Published in 2018
Olympia Publishers
60 Cannon Street
London
EC4N 6NP

Printed in Great Britain

Dedication

To all those who inspired a poem along the way.

Acknowledgments

My thanks to all at Olympia Publishers for their encouragement and help in bringing this collection to print.

Reminiscences on the Dog Walk

Today I dog walked to the spindle tree
Two buzzards mewed overhead.
Earworm "What do you do my lovely
When you're alone in your bed?".
Silhouette from low morning sun
Elongated shadow like a Giacometti figure
Without its worried roughness scratched and raw.
Mindful of that military pastime
Silhouette recognition, enemy kit,
Alternative to what Henry Reed wrote with wit
"Today we have naming of parts"
Info on rifle anatomy starts.
"Remove head dress" Church parade commands;
Girl's groomed hair retained beret's demands.

Hound Stern. Peterborough Hound Show

Stations of the Odyssey

Odysseus Cast Ashore Encounters Nausicaa.

Nausicaa thought him the answer to her dream
This feral man washed up from relentless sea
Shipwrecked by the wrath of Poseidon's storm
Yet in manner far more than he would seem,
A future husband on whose noble knee
Their children would their characters form.
Granted sanctuary in the palace, bathed and clothed,
No parent could refuse him their daughter's hand
Even if home was a distant land,
Now from trauma restored but by some gods loathed,
She little realised this man was married
Until his tales unfold of disasters captive carried.
Yet in the end her dream worked true: contentment
In his son's arms, complete enchantment.

His Grief at The Bard's Tale to The Concern of Nausicaa

Unbeknown to all the gaunt guest
So distressed at the Bard's soft sung story
Of heroics at the siege of Troy
Wept so bitterly at what men destroy
Only grief and gore in war not glory.
(To the queen he had made request
To be returned to his island home
Whence he was headed through the angry foam
And to join his wife unseen for twenty years
For whose presence he had shed many tears.)
Then he unfolded reality, demeanour sad,
Friends lost, condemned to wander not quite mad,
This is Odysseus whose renown precedes
Who against the odds in all succeeds.

His Story of the Event:

Despite his prized nimble wits star-crossed Odysseus
Angered Poseidon leaving dread Cyclops blind
While his costly adventures others remind
He matched the theft of generous Prometheus
(Not forgetful nor a rotter like Theseus)
Travel weary the dark night of the soul in Hades' gloom
Unknowing he fathered in Circe's enchanting room
The son who unwittingly caused his demise.
Calypso's captive stud seven years delayed promise
To return home to loyal Penelope and dismiss
To death her parasite suitors with well-aimed bow
Alpha male let no infidelity arise
With Nausiccaa entranced and who adored
Asking he remember balance of his mind restored.

Cassandra

Cassandra Warns Against the Wooden Horse

Cassandra rent her clothes and spoke
"These avenging Greeks will take all
Total devastation will Troy befall
Humiliated, raped, these walls all broke"
As she eyed the vast wooden horse
"This cavernous belly once op'ed
Will alter and change this War's course
And achieve all the invaders hoped"
Destined to utter prophecies unheeded
Ignored, dismissed, whatever cause pleaded
Captive by Ajax on altar defiled,
Orphaned, enslaved to become exiled,
"Once proud Troy will become a mound
Where little evidence of War is found."

Circe

His Men Are Pigs: He Holds Her at Sword Point

Transformed to pigs the feasting crew
Were unaware of status new
Odysseus with point of sword
Made Circe unweave her spell
Restoring all to the festive board
Then into her power he too fell
Enchanted by such beauty scantily clad
Succumbing to her female charms
Alpha male satisfying her lust
His dreams in danger or turned to dust
Gained mutual pleasure in her arms.
Has life no more than such a moment glad?
So sated it was quite hard to shape
Or formulate plans of escape.

Calypso

Enchanted in Her Bed Chamber

Last one standing Odysseus alone
Spent seven years under Calypso's spell
A stud to satisfy her appetite
Consumed by remorse as day followed night
Held captive in an empty hell
In danger of change to an immortal clone.
He fulfils fate's reason to remain
His native cunning now futile seems
Never to return to his island haunts
Longing for Penelope in vain and taunts
His tortured mind war now distant dreams
Brooding his impotence till come night again.
A sailor might be proud - wife in every port;
But he's a hero marooned for a goddess' sport.

Hades

Dark Night of the Soul Encounters Mother, Ajax and Others

What fate denied the return home?
Was life penance for past mistakes?
Did some quirk in the alignment of her stars,
Keep him from recovering faithful Penelope?
Kindly blind Teiresias his future spilled:
False crew to temptations fall and delays,
Ways to amend, a waiting wife
His palace full of miserable strife,
By his terrible hand each suitor pays,
His mother news of home their eyes tear filled
Until called to Hades' shades where resided
Other women of beauty or for deeds derided
Bearers of threatening sons, matricides, hands all gore
Along with departed colleagues from Troy's war.

Nausicaa

Remember Me

"Never forget me for I gave you life"
Is her farewell of unrequited love, rather
A mother to Odysseus restored, reborn,
Whom she encountered naked and forlorn
Ideal husband acceptable to Father.
'Tis she who enables his return to his wife,
Hero, adventurer, questioning laws,
Master of strategy, blessed with guile,
Borne to survive all times of trial
Champion in war of many a cause.
Yet hope lay in his son she knew
If half the man but as true
As Odysseus to his Penelope
Then theirs true happiness would be.

Epilogue

The Axe Head Challenge: Suitors Slaughtered

Swineherd, dog and nurse knew this stranger
Needing to rescue wife and son from danger.
He knew the knack to string the bow
Flighting the arrow down axe head row
Before pulling a deadly shaft so stern
On each squandering suitor in turn.
Finally, he knew their marriage bed
Must remain in place: this man she wed
Had fashioned it from living wood
Where she conceived and bore their son
Though once to war he would be gone
Twenty years they understood.
Cleared of parasites their lives restored
Unaware of a son born abroad.

Abraham & Isaac

Abraham's knife was poised
Poor Isaac just traumatised
God approved this obedient act
Though it mirrored local rites
Conforming to their strange delights
Then a provided ram in fact
For sacrifice to whom is best
Fulfilling what demand requites
Initiating a new covenant pact.
Thus a new rite is noised
So a tribe temptation fights
To be a cut above the rest.
Patriarchs to a selected race
Can stand before God face to face.

On Eve

I slept well last night freed of dreams
Having taken good measurement
Of an idea, no revelation
Nor uncovered picture. Foundation
Instead on which to build shedding
New light on a speculation
That existed with thought of Eve,
Sketching skeletal shapes to stretch
The mind more feasible forms to fetch
And to realise the possible. Believe
Real reference is needed, pause
To define curves and contours.
Whoso thus might the muse arouse
Abstract remains anonymous.

The Ammonite

Sliced stone the parting gift from souk trader
As if a prehistoric invader
Revealed in polished cross-section
Its evolutionary selection
A debt of many millennial years
When crushed to stone within layers
Of eroded rock a shell embedded
With nautical spiral exposed.
This ammonite its ancient growth displayed
That died out when dinosaurs decayed
Embodies strange lateral beauty grey
Nature's engineering to find a way
For curved predatory mollusc to curl
In safety, witness its home a whorl.

The Artist Reflects

To create is a labour of love not without its own contractions
But to destroy is love's labours lost.
Artist's work once lost nothing proves save the emptiness of
constructions
That challenged and consumption cost.
Should dissatisfaction abide
Not avoiding fear but comfort hide,
For what's lost gains not save despair.
Where there's creativity no fear
Exists. False starts may cause some pain
Yet round it all a freshness can remain.
Creation is prolific so create anew
It hurts to lose what you agonised to do
Like childbirth. Strive till unworkable the clue
For overworking is destruction too

Unselfconscious she dropped by request
Her gown and took up a standing pose
Gathering up luxuriant hair to adorn
Her head with oval smiling face so that
Arms upraised slightly lifted up each breast
Firmly rounded, full nipples coloured rose,
Subtle pubic area just clipped not shorn,
Fecund hips, stomach and abdomen flat,
Thighs and legs long and shapely, thus viewed
Modest model speaks what is left unsaid
Merely lending herself to be instead
Clothed naturally, not naked, nude.
Delighting in those gentle unclad curves
The sculptor in rhythmic bronze preserves.

Reflection on Music on Radio 3

Considered rhythms of Faure's Cantique
Unfold with tenor upon treble lined
Melodious and mellifluous
Musical montage made Racine refined
Never notes superfluous
Nor destined to become antique.
Like a child's bubbles wafted in the wind
Sparkling in the sun shimmering gold
To drift as pinpoints Padstow bound
So the orchestrated choral sound
Alternated to prayer unfold
And the rigours of death rescind.
Notes like a sweep of bubbles glistening
Made for reflective and peaceful listening.

Christ Church Cathedral Organ, Oxford

Chancel Roof, Christ Church Cathedral, Oxford

What stories does this building hold?
Cathedral focus for many souls
Thanks, secrets untold or confessed. Tolls
A bell for hearts that true enfold
A thirst for God plainly seeking,
Enhanced by listening meekly
Pondering the silence weakly
To find the Holy Spirit speaking.
Facts to root us where we belong
Destination of pilgrimage
Shrines to saints martyred in bygone age
Where history unfolds right and wrong.
On all shush descends, prayer
Lifts hearts that stoop to share despair.

Christ Church Cathedral, Oxford. 7, Chancel
Roof

Chancel Roof Vaulting, Christ
Church Cathedral

St Frideswide, Christ Church Cathedral, Oxford

Forbearing caresses, love denied
Frideswide to be a bride declined
Hunted by suitors no Helen she
Hid out of sight, hounded escapee.
Shorn of glory no glory sought
Lifelong gave life with her life bought
Respite for others, mercy, alms.
On the poor she lavished pure charms.
So chaste once chased she lived and died
Making saints from sinners sore tried.
In prayer many would emulate
Her qualities they celebrate
What she missed she never lacked
Living a life with love so packed.

St Frideswide Shrine, Christ Church
Cathedral, Oxford

Frost

Feathers of frost so delicately brushed
Pattern car roofs when caught in sunshine glinting
White icy miniature Arctic with tiny stalagmites
Reaching up a minute forest forming
Crisp canopies covering car screens.
On deeper inspection revealing
Intricacies the human hand would find
Hard to copy. Nature boasts a lively dimension
We cannot see as gentle waves and rivulets
Of cold damp air brush surfaces and freeze
Into fascinating interlocking shapes
With veins, barbs and barbules plus
Looser flues and plumules. No peacock eye
Nor quill with rigid rachis. Just cool softness.

Down the Frosty Lane

Low sun winter weakened filters through a tree screen
Sharp light glistening grass carpeting frosty field
Silent rural contrast to stark trees shadows peeled
To raw silhouette 'gainst darkened town sky if seen
Save school Christmas tree glimmering white
In enclosed city grounds during the night.
Down the lane loudly unsupportive ice cracks
Now the puddle's water is a solid sheet
Too short to slide causes slippery feet
Sending the unwary onto their backs.
Roosting in leafy hedgerow, with a clank
Lifted on whirring wings to woods wild and dank
Disturbed by padding dog sheltered ruffled pheasants
Glide unretrieved. Called back returning dog pants.

Colours

First frost dead leaves carpet the ground
Tunnels of autumn colour are found
Along motorways richer in bright sunshine
Blue sky's only clouds vapour trails told
Planes' passing passage in the cold
Above faded greens, russet and old gold
Rich orange, maple tongues of scarlet fine
No bared branches. Varieties of shape dwindle
All covering fig leaf, delicate maidenhair ore
Crinkled oak, evergreen's darker hues, pointed spindle,
Ancient gingko, slashed ash, crumpled sycamore
Lingering tan-coloured beech, canopy kindle.
Rose tinted dusk will light horizon's frieze
And flame add its background to stark trees.

Off to See Manzu on the no. 30 bus…

There are leaves on the chestnut in Euston Square;
A sign of spring so the tourists appear.
Queues of kids outside Madam Tussauds
While building progresses behind bill-boards.
In Baker Street they search for Holmes.
Back home supermarkets sell garden gnomes.
The waiting traffic is thick
Exhaust fumes make one sick.
Three stations all in a row
From which no steam trains go.
Despite high canopies that caught the smoke
No more smells of burning coal and coke.
Up the hill past Pentonville a fill of art
Beckons from an artist close to the heart.

Come the Morn

Gone is the cuckoo with earlier dawn
Leaving pigeons to clear their throats
Chimney pot perched to megaphone notes
To my bedroom fireplace each morn.
Maybe a laughing yaffle undulated
That in the old walnut tree nested oft.
Spugs chirp. Come a light breeze to waft
Through open window room refreshing
Soft-scented lime blossom, where operated
Last evening myriads of bumble bees.
Adolescent magpies chatter with ease
To thieve our hen food gleaned from threshing.
Cautious squirrels dig but forlorn
Questing nuts once buried in the lawn.

Wisdom

We think of Wisdom as remembering the date
While our forebears remembered to debate
What the event meant.
Now we let Wikipedia comment,
No understanding nor accurate fact:
With Waterloo we mastered Europe's act
But did not occupy it, nor live there.
By 1880 when churches were full and crime low.
Transcending psychology's convolutions
But bowing to man's evolutions
Human nature and reaction to God follow
Victorians were mindful of another fear
That is the beginning of Wisdom.
The Bible is a great compendium.

Reflections on Remembrance

Old Comrades line avenues of poppy plots
Their once full muster now forms up with hollows
Awaiting the silence following clock strike
Big Ben booms bugle beckoning rally follows
Royal visitors meet and greet reckoning ranks
Veterans of their own generation
Symbols of leadership for the nation
Greatcoats warding off the chill less bowler hats
Doffed for simple service and ceremony brief
Like frontline respite all gather to remember;
Gone too mothers of these sons. Still in leaf
Trees around this Abbey green rare for November
Now even those regiments county named
Are culled which once unruly nations tamed.

Female breasts whose sons are safe and sound
Sigh at thoughts of past family not around
Grandchildren of that previous generation
Replace their sons' loss in far flung destination
Of foreign theatres, or in strange seas drowned.
One uncle blown by a bomb but a button was found
In Dunkirk dunes, Military Cross uncited.
Another wounds and valour rewarded post D-Day
In jungle ambush gunned down by bandits lay
Mortally wounded so the records say
Directing continued action by those he trained
'Gainst superior numbers resistance sustained.
Father's hat and belt I wore allegiance plighted
Closing that generation gap by war blighted.

To the Beloved

I love the beloved, what words do I need?
Should I perform some knightly deed?
If that's rescuing damsels in distress
Might that not cause a greater mess?
Yet by the rules of courtly love too
These quests should be dedicated to you
Sporting aloft your special favour
That you such prowess might savour.
In this post-Chaucerian age, we change,
Different arrangements need to engage.
The beloved is loved no love strange
But expressed on more than poet's page,
Thus increasing self-esteem, you learn
Is consolidated where two hearts burn.

Red Rose

From our garden I picked and chose
The most strongly scented I could find
Of perfumed and best coloured kind
For my love a real red rose.
No amount of arias proclaim
Ingrained love reality of life
To stand by and support working wife
Sharing ups and downs without blame.
No Figaro I to try to solve
The vicissitudes of affairs
Changing to whims contrary cares
Of staff meetings short of resolve,
Purveying whisky to restore
Normality to one I adore.

Reflecting on the RSC Tempest

Shipwrecked into Prospero's power
Usurping gang undergo tribulations
To make amends earning forgiveness
They hardly deserved. With God-like control
Spirit world becomes time of trial; they cower,
Remorse tempers hints of perdition. New temptations
Reflect the evil one restless within the soul.
Mercy and love in a Brave New World reside
In young hopes and restored kingdom.
Prospero's conjured company raises
Thoughts of comparison and incompleteness;
Is God needful too of people's praises
Incomplete without his dreams being our fates?
Revenge is blown away when tempest abates.

Squall Over Mull

In Transit

Tasty but short-lived cashew apple
Has rosiness and sweet flavours,
But till well roasted the nut remains
Unpalatable. The husk provides phenol
Irritant when raw but gives contour
Strength to rubber tyres, favours
The quality of protection
In marine paint, and yields medicine.
Amazing extraction by selection
From what others might decline.
This curved cashew proclaims in section
Trinity with flesh, husk, whose nut so fine
Was Resurrected through fire to offer good
Physical, mental, spiritual food.

Dog in the House

I talk to the dog. She's quiet, red
Doesn't answer back. Nowt to hide
At certain words she cants her head
Walk or Hat on, then on t' other side
Dins. On command she heads for bed.
I tell her what I'm doing will provide.
Watching with longing eyes unblinking
She listens, sitting patiently, on her rump
Not on her haunches, as if thinking.
Will she come shooting, retrieve? I jump
In play towards her bone busied:
She circles fast until we are dizzied,
Tail tucked down, but quite a friend;
Now go, on my dinner attend.

Midwives to the Mini

Tall orange robots bend affectionately
Dedicated to metal frames' assembly,
Which embryos become a new creation
Through co-ordinated dexterity
Piecing components with red hot fusion.
Elegant movements, silent synchronisation,
Performance programmed to measured pace,
Interlock displaying a certain grace.
Midwives to floor pans: no emotion is shown
But a corporate character of their own,
KUKAs wave underframes overarm
With a dancer's ease, poise and charm,
ABBs with grippers and welding gun
Place parts to join as each Mini is done.

Long-lived 50's child, inspiration
Issigonis' brainchild, iconic to a generation
A new millennium saw resurrection
To match an age become obese
Morris Mini Minors cease
Along with Austin Minis, BMC's
Branding changing to British Leyland,
Rover and other marques, BMW and
A compilation of former names stop,
Well known in the old body shop.
Robot assisted automation makes
Successor variants that four thousand takes
Replacing twenty-eight thousand before
Who laboured by hand on the shop floor.

Sonnet: The Foundling Hospital

No more doorstep dumped pulling feint hearts
Foundlings at last given hope of fresh starts
Regardless whether whelp of high born or tarts.
Sir Thomas Coram recruited others to play parts,
Surrogate father with philanthropists;
Hogarth's horrors of Gin Lane's low life mists
Roused their concern to act, whilst Handel's scores
Encouraged instrumentalists to perform;
Boys serve the colours with music their norm
Girls in service have better futures than whores.
Chance of survival beyond five and good health
Gained admittance if no black ball, not wealth,
Barred the way or white replaced red. Few minions'
Strange tokens left in hope redeemed re-unions.

Mindfulness

Amuse a muse by producing
Life reflecting or inducing
A sense of being, point in time,
In form of plaster or in rhyme.
Her response in time will follow
Feelings heartfelt far from hollow
Or her very being offered pure
Is there in the round to explore.
Pleasant presence pleasing personality
Her company brightens working day
Drives insularity away.
Present in the moment breathes tranquility
Mindful such moments feed
As each in other finds a need.

Very present in the moment
Reflects on our being and feeds
Thoughts leading to an inner calm
Finding a new tranquility
Honing a new ability
Prayer as an inward balm
Recognising Christ meets our needs
Life is quality not ferment.
Mindfulness sees obvious links
Like spiritual reflection
Recognises a connection
Between what is and what one thinks.
How good to realise sense of place
Such stability no disgrace.

In the Atlas region

Here High Atlas held the heaven,
On quest mighty Hercules strode.
Torrents westward wash the earthen hills,
Baked brick houses and mud walls erode.
Garden of roses with aroma fills
The air, where all those olives ripen
Before harvest from coloured groves
Of silvery green flicked by the wind,
Stretching up terraced valleys.
Berber ovens yield toasted loaves.
Rocks for pigment prove worthy find.
Round La Roseraie the work force rallies,
Tillers talk until they homeward go
And to a carpet add another row.

To Marrakech…

The road moans to Gatwick whence the flight
Was an eclectic mix of families and nations,
Only glimpsing Saharan dunes undulate from height
As we banked to land for late lunch of strange rations.
In Marrakech as mopeds weaved drivers at roundabouts
Cautiously edged. Street might lead to marabouts.
Uneven paths interlace medieval medina where ancient crafts
Were plied with dexterous skills, or compelling wafts
Of spices tickled the nose. Bright dyes earthily sourced
Colour skeins of wool and silk for kaftans and carpets flung
Drying in the sun as do the tanned hides. Camel bones forced
Into wood made marquetry, nothing wasted, and butchers hung
Their meat along the way. Laden scooters pushed and surged
And those minding their wares throughout the souk sales urged.

…And Beyond

Dappled light in gardens of bamboo where water courses flow
Through blossom to a paradise of ponds finds small frogs croak
Large on lily-pads, prolific as any Monet's paintings evoke.
Nature's colours are repeated in Taureg scarves of indigo.
Thin men in their jellabas like hobbits billow along the road
As their womenfolk in their sirwals, serouals and kaftans,
broad.
Younger girls enjoy greater freedom: boys together band and
stand
In contrast to those rural families who work the land,
Where goats graze up argan trees (drought defying) to spit
The nuts for human use and sweet ointments when crushed and
split.
We cross desert, wadis, oases, olives, citrus-like malls
To reach the port of crowded fishing boats their catch in stalls.
Here midst development the Atlantic batters the shore
And the old deserted bastions salute the Portuguese no more.

Family Gathering

The corps of cousins collect to meet
Consuming canapés and champagne
At Hoare's Bank who host this treat
Encouraging each and all to regain
Old acquaintanceships and newly greet
Others where encounters dormant lain
Find common ground in social round
Of familial company gathering views
With relaxed purpose to explore news,
Activities or merely astound
With achievements or inventions.
Promises of good intentions
May be kept or regretted next year
Depending how well each and all wear.

2016

It's been a year of interesting travel
(No bad thing before you unravel).
We took car and dog to Eire by ferry
To tour and more round the Ring of Kerry.
By plane to taste Morocco where of course
We explored Atlas by well-behaved horse,
Dined on fish in Essaouira's port
From Atlantic waters freshly caught.
Saw goats spitting argan nuts from the trees
Then gathered for oil your health to please.
In the souks discovered dyed silks all bound
Hanging in skeins to dry above ground.
Cornwall promised family, surf and sun
Once buried church from sand dunes won.

The Row, An Insight

Wave of undeserved invective strikes unseen
Across the table under where children cower
Bent on their own distractions. This no shower
More of a storm, unleashed tsunami of spleen.
Busy on the floor small four try to ignore,
Occupied, avoiding detection, pretending
Experiments, becalmed under outbursts of rage;
Unalarmed mother is driven to disengage,
Not heart rending, relationship beyond mending,
All aftermath is tentative and sore.
Calm in the face of such rejection
Balm is found in maternal affection
For four needing love by anger shaken
Until new life looms for one forsaken.

Temple Carol Service 2016

To hear Temple carols they queued well filed
While a little girl skipped outside,
And remember Christ the manger-bound child,
The Magi, and where shepherds abide,
Inspired chants, stories familiar or mild,
Soloist in triforium spied,
Folk songs, versions jazzed up or wild,
Celebrating a taste of Christmastide.
Within the organ sets the mood
Sacred pieces to inspire;
Prayers kindle spiritual fire
Following readings all understood.
The national spiritual eclipse applied
Where sacred and secular collide.

Queuing Outside Temple Church, London

Tallis Sonnet

Rood screen of harmonious sound
Lifts souls to eternal embrace
Church full filled with musical grace,
Passionate setting your hand I found.
Words become instruments of voice
Soaring in Allegri on high
Transporting - balloons in the sky -
Capturing where hearts rejoice
Emotions no more mortal bound
Responsorial in great taste
Presence not to leave in haste
Lingers repeat on Holy ground.
Hands held no need for us to speak
Love enfolds sublime levels seek.

Sussex Modernists Anticipated

Sussex Modernists now show
Paintings of such colour and verve
With subjects touching a raw nerve;
Bohemian attitudes sow
Relationships where others don't go
Which Victorians didn't know
But practiced with less gay abandon.
Intimate and intellectual
Interests proved heady fuel
Along such communal lines
For all to put a hand on
Each other's desires and designs.
No social challenges ducked
Convention and art rules bucked.

Water from Rock

Layers of settling sediment with different tone
Over many millennia smothered old rock,
By sheer weight compressed to porous sandstone.
Minerals dissolve, accumulate, blocking water in faults
Until the crusted deposits on strata edges were struck
By Moses' staff; water flowed on dislodging the salts.
In wadis hungry Israelite refugees pluck
The white crystallised flowers from the Rumph plant
Now enjoyed by camels but once as manna food stock
Nourishing a nation that at God would rant.
While atop Sinai strange natural action
Produces letter-like patterns, the citation
Of law giving tablets for social application.
This practical explanation gave spiritual direction.

Calgary Bay, Mull

Old Testament Sinai

The wind at the fissures worries, rock face streaking,
Finding out cracks, sand-blasting and seeking
Between laminates, round corners devouring,
Loaded like carborundum scouring,
Leaving niches and cornices until all tumble.
Before this strongest element stone will crumble,
Carved, reduced to dust. Continuing creation
God formed Adam from this dust provided,
Breathed life, ruarch, into him and divided
To make Eve to multiply each generation.
After the wind to utter silence is Elijah alert.
The wind stays, sweeps rushing o'er the desert
Causing Hosea on Israel's future to reflect
That it's she whom God might blast and reject.

The Burning Bush

Moses shoeless stood on holy ground,
The burning bush unconsumed found:
Sign that God would deliver from bondage
A populous people, slavery their wage.
Though Moses daren't look directly for shame
When God spoke to reveal his name,
Future and present, a basic verb, will and am.
This bush symbolises the Virgin born lamb,
Whose unquenchable flame reaches into our spiritual life.
Fraxinella, bramble, monastery bound round Sinai cliff
Is called Rubus Sanctus, not the gas plant Diptam,
Dictamnus Albus, with too short-lived flame,
This glory, uncreated energies of God, shows His face,
Logos, His Word, and saving grace for a chosen race.

Skye and Eigg from Calgary, Mull